Loving Me More so I can Love You Better

Five Exercises for Couples who want a Creative and
Adventurous Approach to Improving their Marriage

Ed Golden

Foreword

RICK STASI

About this book

A psychiatrist walks down the street and runs into one of his professional peers. He greets the other doctor with *"You're fine. How am I?"*

Relationships. The onset of visuals and perceptions— "best foot forward" and the like. The fragile first impressions of "How *you* doin'?" when what we really mean is "How *my* doin'"?

There is a vulnerability in the human psyche that teeters on turbulence. All we want is to be acknowledged, accepted, and understood—and to reciprocate, for a hopefully "happily ever after!"

There! That's satisfying! That's endgame, right? Not so fast...

In recent studies (FORBES Advisor, 2024) 75% of individuals and couples cited lack of commitment as the reason for their divorce. This was the most common cause of a marriage ending, exceedingly even infidelity. Shocking!

Loving Me More So I Can Love You Better is Rev. Dr. Ed "Doc" Golden's five-step guide to healthier, happier and more prosperous marriages, no matter what stage of relationship building you may be involved in.More importantly, ***Loving Me More So I Can Love You Better*** is a workbook! It is a ground-zero, no holds barred, mirror-imaging course that will enlighten you before you leap into another's life. Discover how to be your best "you" in order to bring out the best in someone else.

Roll up your sleeves. Clear your mind. Leave your ego at the door and work Doc Golden's five-step workbook! Watch how hard it works for you—and maybe, just maybe, someone you love.

***

About the author

My friend Doc Golden is an accomplished counselor, chaplain, US Navy Vietnam veteran and life coach.

He is an ordained Unity Minister and addictions counselor. (Truth to tell, Doc has so many accomplishments, awards, and accolades, it could fill this book.) He's even taken me aside a time or two. For that, I'm a better person.

Doc Golden has been published in magazines and periodicals on topics of Personal and Spiritual Development, Motivation and Goal Achievement, Addiction Recovery, Family Marriage issues, in articles, poetry, programs, and books. His previous book is titled, *From Skid Row to the Front Row, or When Drugs and Poverty Stop Working.*

Doc has been married to his best friend, Susan, for 34 years, and together they have three sons and enjoy making things for charity. He is an avid golfer and directs or helps direct golf tournaments for several of his charitable organizations.

***

Rick Stasi is an artist, author and performer residing in the Greater Kansas City area. He thinks Doc is "tops!"

Preface

A Perspective of Marriage

A philosophical framework is a set of values, ideals, beliefs, behaviors, and customs that have become the classic way people conduct their marriage. Some of these come from expectations and historical patterns families have adopted and passed along, or they could be a product of what we think of what others have shared. There is the "falling in love stage", which is probably more emotional, romantic, or imagined in the "counting period". Many couples feel an intense desire to strut their newfound treasure with anyone and everyone to show the ecstatic feelings just discovered. For a time, this over-the-top behavior exists to the extent of maturity the couple has obtained. At some point their toes will touch the ground and they will begin to realize how much energy it takes to maintain this much momentum, and reality is going to come into place and remind them that while they are locked up in the world of romantic bliss, that there is a world in which they still have to conform. Things like school, jobs, paying the rent and car payment can't simply be ignored.

Then the wedding comes into the planning stage and thoughts go more toward the event, and not as much about individual goals and dreams. There will be continued dates in which the discussion will be flooded with the details of the vows. There will be a time with the wedding planner, the D.J., minister, bridesmaids, groomsmen, ring bearer and flower girl. This takes up time and energy, along with the regular life functions mentioned, so once all the arrangements are made, there will be an adjustment period requiring them to be present at the ceremony. Pretty soon then comes the big wedding day when customarily the bride and groom are separated from each other for a bit until they find themselves at the altar, ready to make the commitment to a life shared together. Even after saying "I do" they will still not be able to get their minds wrapped around all that just happened, but soon it will become evident.

The reception is over, everyone has gone home, and Mr. And Mrs. are finally alone in their room, and for the first time are faced with the identity theft that occurred earlier. Whatever previous goals, dreams and ideals that were set in concrete are up for possible changes. The same money for tuition may now be getting spent on household expenses, or the time needed to attend to those things will now seem to have disappeared. Initially each will say that it's okay knowing some things would have to be given up, but in the mind of the beholder, there is an afterthought, "I'll get back to it very soon, so it's okay for now", one fact stands out clearly: there is no going back to the way it used to be.

The roles might not include the night out with the guys or girls. The Wednesday golf game may fade into mowing the lawn after work. The most comes when Jim and Lucy become "dad" and "mom" and it takes a very strong marriage to navigate all this. It may be years before either of them gets back to attaining some or any of the goals for life previously set. Building strength of character and being authentic will make the mark.

Contents

Part One:

Setting the Stage

Chapter One

Who Needs This?

M arriage has long since been much, much more than two people of the correct age who fall in love, get married, have children, and live in society on main street.

In my own life, I found that when I woke up at the age of 29, going on 14, I didn't have anything more to work with than the values and concepts that I had at the age of 13. It doesn't take much to figure out what the success of my relationships were. There were many, very unhealthy, unproductive practices that left me wondering after five years of recovery, if I wanted to have another relationship, or be a monk on a mountain top in Tibet.

The ensuing years led me to a discovery of personal identity, esteem, and dignity. I found when I had sufficiently developed emotionally, mentally, and spiritually, that I had something worth sharing, and I would no longer be willing to share it with someone else who did not have a very good idea about who they are, and what they want in life. It's difficult going through adolescence when you're nearly 30 years old. I have done enough research, pre-marital, and marriage counseling to know that my experience is in no way isolated. It doesn't take chemical addiction to cause problems in a marriage, although that certainly will. What causes the real problem is people who are addicted to someone else for the fulfillment of their needs.

Among other professional experiences, I taught the FOCIS (Focus on children in separation) program for family court for 15 years to couples going through divorce. The content of this writing is based on decades of helping people find the love in their heart and find that special someone who resonates with the values, habits, beliefs, and life goals to build a successful life together.

One thing that doesn't belong in a healthy relationship is complacency. I had a client who was a nurse. She came to see me because her license was up for suspension as she had been found using some of the sedatives and antidepressants from the medicine chest in the office. She had been working for this doctor for over 20 years, and had never had any issues, particularly with medications. She told me she had a husband and daughter who waited on her at home each night to get dinner ready almost at once as she got home. She mentioned passing a park on the way home each day, and wished she could stop and spend a few minutes to relax and take a short walk before returning home. In essence she felt like a human doing instead of a human being and took the medications to quit her anxiety along with shear boredom of the daily routine. We worked on her self-worth and setting some new boundaries for her duties at home. She became delighted with the idea of having the freedom to stop by the park on her way home for a few minutes to unwind from medical practice, and she found it was a lot of fun to feed the birds in the park. On Wednesday she would call home as she left the office and tell her husband or daughter to put on the hot dogs, and she would be home soon. She also began to change clothes at the office. When she came to work in the morning, she would dress in her uniform, and upon leaving, reinstate her personal attire. It changed her whole being in terms of how she felt about herself at home and at work, and others quickly noticed the difference in her step. She was able to keep her license, and her marriage, but more importantly, she kept her self-respect.

In my work with couples who are getting ready to blend families from previous marriages, I've discovered it is important to avoid identity theft. Addressing this issue helps build a family unit rather than them becoming a fragmented group. For couples just getting married for the first time, it happens when the baby comes. Instead of Mark and Phyllis, now we have "mommy" and "daddy." While this is relatively harmless for the short term, very soon couples need to remember who they are, and not be relegated to their job role in the family. Dignity, identity, and purpose give each person autonomy, so their person doesn't become the one who merely does something.

When it comes to remarriage with children, I highly recommend family counseling. Counseling helps to prevent problems. Therapy, on the other hand, is what you need if you neglect necessary counseling. There should be consideration for the children who are shifted back and forth from one home to another on visiting schedules. I strongly recommend that each child has a sign on their bedroom door with their name on it, and somewhere in the main living area of the house, a family picture arrangement. It is beneficial for the family to have a written agreement about duties and boundaries, so no one gets lost or feels like they don't have a place. The term "step" should not be used to identify an individual. Call them by their given name. Things like daddy-daughter dances don't have the word "step" in them, and I suggest the term be dropped universally. I met my daughter for the first time when she was 18 and I still refer to her as my daughter.

The intent here is to give workable and effective solutions to the issues that haunt people in working toward achieving success in their relationship. When couples come away from the experiences outlined in the book, they will have rid themselves and their relationship of a lot of lies, pain, hurt, and shame that has been preventing them at some level from realizing all their marriage can be. Practice of the exercises here may raise more questions than it will answers, but you will have a blueprint for the future, and learn the value of periodic checkups that keep marriage fun and growing. The level of intimacy will be deepened, and fear of confrontation and conflict will be diminished. Traditional roles in marriage, and all that goes with them, will be replaced by healthy boundaries, and more equitable cooperation between spouses. These exercises will instill an understanding of the proactive care needed in marriage.

There are no magic tricks to making a successful marriage. It takes a lot of energy, hard work, and many trials and errors. Perhaps just being willing to make mistakes and work them out with your mate is a step above what a lot of people experience in a lifetime of marriage. Couples will come away with a set of tools designed to help them recognize challenges and progress in their relationships. The hope is to face the relationship with maturity and freedom instead of fear of losing the relationship for being honest.

The process in this book is one of individual exploration and sharing the findings with each other. It is an experience which begins with trust building and ends with a new commitment. What is in between is what the exercises are about. The elements have been constructed to be both exploratory and fun. There will be an atmosphere that will breed both openness and intimacy and show that you can live together and complement each other. This program will enhance the imagination, creative abilities, and problem-solving skills.

Chapter Two

What Went Wrong?

The divorce rate in our country is alarming. Statistics show that fifty-four percent of marriages fail in the first ten years. The results are worse than simply two people who no longer live together and pay lawyers and courts hefty fees. The pressures of both partners working full time jobs, while trying to maintain the traditional roles of man and wife are leaving people feeling frustrated, betrayed, angry, and hurt. My first marriage ended because she didn't want to be a navy wife and it was the 60's and he had a corvette. Actually, it really ended before it started. I was 19 and had been in the navy for two years, and she was 17 and wanted to get away from home. Six years later there were two boys, but having children didn't create enough value for the marriage to survive. While I was at sea, infidelity and my being gone caused the ultimate demise of our relationship. I divorced her just before going to Vietnam. During my deployment, the kids were supposed to be staying with her parents, but during that time she left with no explanation to the kids. It takes some very special people to make marriage work when you don't live together and have up to six months without any physical contact. After the divorce, twelve years went by with no communication from her. When she did decide to try re-entering our sons' lives, it was without contrition. She never took responsibility for what she did, and the boys distanced themselves from any real relationship with her. It would be some years later that I would have a renewed vision for married life and be able to make better choices in relationships.

Married people wonder, "What's wrong? We did it the way we were supposed to, and it just didn't work for us." We have created an emotional and financial monster with something called child support and alimony. Recent statistics show that only a little over half of single parents today are receiving the amount of child support that was the court ordered.

This sets up several serious problems other than the fiscal disaster of splintered, low-income families. The children grow up feeling like they are a burden to the absent parent. Parents have been alienated from their children, and the children grow up thinking this is normal. They also grow up thinking it is normal to feel the way they do about themselves. They grow up, get married, repeat what they know, and the cycle continues.

I don't believe the way it has typically been done ever really worked. I do believe that society has become hypnotized with archaic, autocratic, and patriarchal ideas of what marriage is supposed to be. Marriage is a spiritual institution, and its core needs to reflect values rather than moral laws set up in older times. People don't play roles in marriage as if they were a job assignment. It doesn't mean one goes out and earns a salary and one stays home and does the cooking and cleaning. In today's world, it means that these duties are shared according to who has time and ability. My wife does the laundry. I fold it and put it away. We each have rooms we clean and dust, and I go pick up food when she doesn't feel like cooking. The good news amid the disastrous conditions of today's marriage arena is that I think finally, people realize that marriage is not a role play, but two people sharing their lives who have some common goals, are intelligent, creative, loving, and fully capable of being a whole person on their own. They are also discovering that there are a lot of people who have equally found their wholeness who make good marriage partners. Fortunately, I can now relate to this, as we have been married now for over 34 years and continue to grow and share everything life brings together.

There are many external factors that can affect a good marriage. Substance abuse, mental illness, child abuse, various forms of abuse, poor education, low income, and other factors of living in a compulsive, competitive, aggressive society have also taken their toll on marriages. Even people with educations and good incomes find themselves beset by career stress, lack of recreation, and loss of personal identity. Not everyone suffers from any or all these things, but it is possible with rigorous honesty, treatment, and continued understanding of the pitfalls, it is possible to overcome the obstacles of any condition and have a great relationship.

Unhealthy Relationships, Patterns, and Roles

Unhealthy relationships form or develop when certain conditions are present. Most of these conditions are healthy characteristics that are taken to extremes of importance; hence, they fall out of balance. We can become compulsive or obsessive about a particular aspect of the relationship if we are short sighted enough to think that focusing on just one or two aspects are all it takes to make a relationship work. People who are bound to role playing in a marriage find they can perpetuate what is unhealthy but lack courage or direction to change it.

Relationships can begin to dissolve if one of the partners becomes tired of playing the role or begins to develop healthy ideas about relationships because of entering therapy or some type of recovery program. People can also go amiss when one factor becomes more of a focus instead of keeping the big picture in mind. And when the spiritual core is obscured, things deteriorate quickly, and people find themselves in a great deal of unhappiness and distress. In trying to manage the relationship without good tools, we can develop addictions.

We get addicted to security-never enough love, understanding, or money.

Never enough emotional, psychological, material security because of the underlying feeling of unworthiness. Some people think if they can get enough of one or the other that everything else will be okay.

We get addicted to sensations provided by alcohol or other drugs, food, or sex.

They'll make us feel okay for a while; they'll make us feel secure. But the addiction takes over and makes you feel like you don't have enough of the magical "make me feel good instantly" experience. You fear losing this security, so you become compulsively addicted.

We become addicted to power and control-This can traverse into needing to have control at any price over the fear of losing everything. We seek the power to create feelings of worth and lovability.

Doing a thorough Relationship Resume (covered in Chapter 7) will help uncover unhealthy patterns before entering an intimate and deep-seated relationship. Our pattern of choosing someone has primarily developed from our sense of attraction, which tends to more physical than spiritual, so many of the signals don't register in the conscious realm and get smothered by the romantic and emotional attachments we have for one another. We may have some pre-conceived ideas that we rule out by reflecting on past relationships but won't be aware of those we have yet to experience. The urging of this text is to explore every facet of being with a special person and all that comes with that. We all have a history, and often couples neglect to explore those things out of fear. The bottom line is, if our ability to choose a mate isn't developed, and we haven't done the repair work to gain a healthy perspective, we will likely repeat the same relationship choices that don't work. We see so many people who "marry" their parents. Without any new data, we will continue to use the same values and choices we always have because we are comfortable with them, and it seems safer to go with what we know, and not explore new options. This can come from our fear that we won't be acceptable to the other person as opposed to evaluating whether they are right for us. There couldn't be a better reason to continue this journey through the book than to change the old familiar patterns. After all, that is why you bought this book.

Here are some signals of unhealthy patterns, habits, or beliefs that could ultimately destroy a couple's capacity to be happy together:

1. <u>Thinking more about the relationship than anything else</u>. Not taking time to consider personal needs and goals. Both people exist for the needs of relationship and abandon their own. This fosters secret resentments and fears.

2. <u>Avoiding relationships, fearing the expected pain</u>.
When people think that they will be harmed by a relationship, they are looking at the wrong thing. It is not the bond of two people that causes pain, but rather the unhealthy sharing of the idea that people can't have love without pain.

3. <u>Having to know where your partner is at all times</u>. This is a real prison of fear. When we are so insecure that we can't allow another person

the freedom to do anything alone, we'll never be comfortable living with ourselves.

4. Jealous and hurt if our partner notices someone of the opposite sex. One can feel a sense of ownership, and genuinely fear a loss of ownership if the partner appreciates the appeal of someone.

5. Needing undue praise, fishing for compliments, and feeling hurt and rejected if not given. No amount of praise or compliments will ever fill the void of emptiness a person may feel. It is emotionally exhausting for the partner. This expectation will also cause feelings of inadequacy because they can't provide enough praise to make the other happy.

6. Seeking identity from the relationship. This is power by association. Some people feel that prestige is important, so they value who they are with, more than themselves. They lose their personal identity.

7. Needing a sense of security – When this happens, people look to their partner as the ultimate solution or salvation. Here is where gender roles become important. This demand can make one feel guilty for not playing their part.

8. Rearranging each other's lives to meet the needs of the other.
There is always an intense feeling of emptiness, and the mistaken idea is that one is not giving enough to another, so individual needs get excluded as secondary.

9. Avoiding conflict to keep the relationship intact. Peace at any price means more pain and a complete lack of honesty. There is no skill in this relationship to solve problems, so they simply get swept under the rug.

10. Making unkept promises to yourself and each other. This is how commitment is lost. There is no integrity or purpose left. Each begins

to make excuses for themselves and devalues the meaning of the words spoken.

11. <u>Believing that you cannot live without each other.</u> This is a sure death sentence. People have forgotten that they had a life before that other person came into their grip.

12. <u>Knowing it is time to release their partner but just can't let them go.</u> Losing the other person feels like a death if a large percentage of personal identity is wrapped up in them. It also means admitting having made a decision that wasn't the best.

13. <u>Continuing your commitment, believing that your mate's unacceptable behavior will go away, eventually</u>. The person who tolerates unacceptable behavior will to that extent become responsible for it.

14. <u>Bonding is only felt during sexual acts.</u> Considering that even the most amorous people can consummate the sexual act for a maximum of an hour per day, there will be many remaining hours of feeling abandoned. It takes true meaning and intimacy for connection to be present outside of the act of sex.

15. <u>Measuring the degree of your love by the degree of your torment and pain</u>. Our music industry often affirms this misconception. Try to find more than a few songs per day played on the radio that say something about how love feels warm and good. (note: if you play a country and western record backwards, you get your wife back, your pickup truck stays on the road, and you sober up).

16. <u>Feeling fully alive only when in a close relationship.</u> This is a real testimony to how much you think of yourself and how comfortable you are being you.

Role playing in relationships brings out some undesirable characteristics in people and gives some very unhealthy payoffs. The following will show how these roles perpetuate unhealthy relationships.

Role: The Little Girl or Little Boy

Characteristics: playing helpless, innocent, indecisive, immature, irresponsible; egocentric, manipulative, dependent, phony, fear

The Payoff: fulfilling security by expecting someone else to be responsible for our well-being.

Role: The Peacemaker

Characteristics: Runs from one person to another explaining and controlling needs. Covering, protecting, in denial, people pleasing, approval-seeking, hypocritical, dishonest, guilty, avoidance, perfectionism, manipulation

The Payoff: fulfulling security by controlling relationships.

The Role: The Banker

Characteristics: pays the bills, addicted to control, recognition-seeking, inconsiderate, over-achieving, controlling, workaholic, uninvolved in family life, possessive, false sense of pride, intolerance, selfishness, providing monetarily becomes currency for making demands in family life

The Payoff: fulfilling security by needing to be the provider of resources.

Role: The Victim

Characteristics: feels misunderstood and mistreated, pity, vying for attention, helpless, innocent, isolating, passive, sulking, dependency, manipulation, blaming, rejection, inadequacy

The Payoff: fulfilling security through looking to be rescued.

Role: The Martyr

Characteristics and attitudes: making others feel guilty, saintly, stoic, suffering, noble, dishonesty, self-pity, false sense of pride.

The Payoff: fulfilling security through personal sacrifice.

Role: The Fixer

Characteristics and attitudes: "You can't do it as good as I can"; needing to be in charge, believing they can do it better than others, controlling, takes over, nosey, disrespectful, nagging, impatience, intolerance.

The Payoff: fulfilling security through creating a false sense of being needed.

Role: The Rescuer

Characteristics and attitudes: self-serving, possessive, over-protective, self-righteous, insecure, manipulative, codependent, egocentric.

The Payoff: fulfilling security through being number one and indispensable.

Role: The Boss

Characteristics and attitudes: control addiction, creates deadlines, distant, demanding, wants production and reliability, efficient, cost-oriented, emotionally uninvolved, perfectionistic.

The Payoff: fulfilling security through managing the family like a board meeting.

Role: The General

Characteristics and attitudes: the ultimate commander, runs the family militaristically, is the judge and jury, their word is final, rigid, obedience to them is key, uncompromising, they know best, egocentric, intolerant.

The Payoff: fulfilling security through dominating and suppressing others.

Role: The Macho

Characteristics and attitudes: never hurt, "unfeeling", won't express a range of emotions, seems undisturbed, cool, uncaring, materialistic, arrogant, intolerant, belittling, braggart, vain.

The Payoff: fulfilling security through faking superiority.

Role: The Feminist

Characteristics and attitudes: Hates men, rejects her femininity as a sign of weakness, argumentative, blaming, competitive, rejecting, cold, know-it-all, resentment, intolerance, anger, wants to re-invent the world.

The Payoff: fulfilling security through being competitive and abu-
sive.

We can all find ourselves somewhere in this list at one time or another in
life. This is an opportunity to examine where we are, not where we'd like to
be. The healthy person will not grow deeply entrenched into any of these
lifestyles and will not want to have an intimate relationship with anyone
who shows these patterns of behavior or belief. This is some work that
must be done to grow into a healthier, happier, and more loving partner,
and there is no shortcut. We can't wish away our old values. We need to be
fully aware of them and not only know we need to change them but recast
a vision of what life will look like when we do.

Chapter Three

Blueprint For the Future

I have done many seminars on relationships, parenting, family values, and personal development, and in talking with and collaborating with people I discovered several things. One of which is that married couples today are trying their best to build a contemporary, workable, and functional relationship based on what they found out from their parents and friends. I find that people suffer from lack of understanding about what it takes to make a marriage work, because they learned what they know from people who came out of the industrial, technological, and space-age revolutions. There has never been a people revolution in this world, and it is now time that we had one. I find that people are hungry for something new that will work for them. The old value system worked well when only the needs of the system were important. Now people are beginning to recognize their own value in this society and are no longer willing to just sit back and become another statistic in the divorce court. I find in working with couples that sometimes things become too ordinary and routine, and in the day-to-day struggle to deal with life, lose sight of why they picked their partner. Not that there is necessarily anything wrong with their partner, but with time, the identity crisis occurs. When Tom and Nancy become mom and dad, they perhaps became lost in the overall meaning of their relationship. My wife and I have been married 34 years and we have a dinner date every Sunday. When she volunteers all day Friday, it's my turn to "cook" dinner, and thankfully there are many places to get takeout for whatever seems to fit her appetite. It could be something right on her way home, but she's tired and really appreciates that I will go find her delicacy and bring it to her. Complacency may seem very comfortable and predictable, but a little distraction from something different has a magic way of keeping the spark glowing.

While I abhor statistics, I can't argue with those concerning the number of failed marriages. I can, however, see the usefulness of those numbers. They show just how many couples can expect to have a good marriage without knowing what they are doing. It would have the same rating for succeeding as trying to build a Volkswagen without technical manual and a lot of training. People who do receive the training become much better mechanics in relationships. One of the things that is extremely helpful for people with this type of experience is to find out they are not alone. They discover that their communications problems are universal enough that books have been written about them. They also find out they don't have to stay stuck. There is much they can do about the problems they are facing. This book embraces those needs. It doesn't matter how long a couple has been married, or how many problems they face. If they are willing to enter this experience with an open mind and have a genuine desire to improve the quality of their relationship, they are in good company.

The right setting is vital. When completing the exercises in this book, I recommend you be away from the usual distractions. As much as possible, it is useful to emotionally detach from the challenges of bills, children, in-laws (if anyone ever had this problem), so total attention is on the work. There is wisdom to learn to help solve the problems that have been set aside. Perhaps you and your spouse are overdue for some time to totally focus on the work at hand.

The conclusions are quite simple. If marriage is going to be the kind of experience people deserve, there must be healthy, workable, and practical materials and experiences for people to engage in, which helps them discover what they need to know.

It's important to identify the difference between thinking and feeling. Individuals and couples must learn how to stop stuffing their feelings because they don't think they are important. People have been taught to ignore feelings in our society long enough. It's time people learnt that feelings are not facts, and there is nothing wrong with a person who feels differently than his or her mate. This can be complimentary and a learning experience.

Couples must divorce from the unhealthy and unproductive habits and beliefs they have about marriage due to the molds that have been imposed by society. They must also rid themselves of self-hatred and old beliefs or the marriage will suffer emotional and mental infection, which robs it of its dignity and courage.

Married people need to keep passion alive in their marriage by mixing play with romance, spiritual growth, fair fighting, commitment, and a renewal of that commitment on a regular basis. Couples also conclude from this experience the need for regular personal and marital inventories, which maintains an awareness of the current conditions.

I can see clients all day, every day, who are simply unhappy with their marriage. They are full of suspicion, anger, blame, confusion, and guilt. They feel ripped off that the idea of marriage should be something they can understand, and yet so many prove they don't have the faintest idea of how to consummate a healthy relationship.

People are more than willing to work on their marriage if they have a safe, healthy, and comfortable environment in which to do the work. It is impossible for anyone to work on a problem while they are buried in it. People need to be able to step back and look from a non-threatening place of objectivity. When people are in a place where they feel emotionally safe, they will be able to face confrontation without feeling a need to defend themselves. They learn that different doesn't translate to wrong. They also discover that confrontation is a very healthy and important part of conflict resolution. Too many people want the problem solved without ever addressing it. It is also paramount here to mention that you cannot treat the problem if all you have in front of you is the symptom(s).

The amount of time and energy spent on communication is well worth what it takes to clear up misconceptions and myths about misunderstandings. Couples can learn to allow their differences to become complimentary in their relationship rather than oppositional.

The most important conclusion is that nothing is going to change in a marriage until the plan changes. Nothing happens by accident, and whether people are aware of it, each has a responsibility for the way the marriage turns out. If a couple doesn't know where they are going, any path will work. If there isn't a plan for the marriage to get well and stay that way, it will relapse into something that neither partner is going to be happy with. If a marriage is going to be a growing organism, the work described in this book is going to be a vital part of the growth of that relationship. It is a healthy couple who seek a marriage counselor or attain outside guidance.

This is no different than taking care of physical health. Regular check-ups ensure ongoing wellness.

I also conclude that couples come away from a session together having clarity of the needs, a new perspective, a deeper commitment, and a greater level of personal esteem than they had at first.

Normal is a Setting on a Clothes Dryer

The idea of creating something new and different requires new and different thinking. The normal most people grew up with and applied meant the routine was normalized and customs and rituals followed that nuclear families have repeated generation after generation. Traditions are good as far as they go, as long as they are healthy and not practiced necessarily because that's the way it has always been done. Many families have remained in the rut of always doing what they always did, even if it was boring, pointless, and unproductive. Repeating family rituals can be co-dependent, and a move to avoid retribution for changing something that had no real purpose. Why do families get ready for the holidays, even though too much money was spent on it last year and in previous years, and the same food eaten because it was there, not because it was enjoyed, let alone having three helpings? Do people really enjoy the feeling of overeating and sitting in a dazed hump on the couch and don't feel like moving; isn't that what is done every year? It can become about everyone indulging in their own egotistical sauces.

Maybe it's time for some new traditions! During the pandemic, people experienced a "new normal" being quarantined and not being able to indulge in the usual traditions. While that had a downside to it, it led to finding new and different ways of doing things. When the pandemic was over, some continued doing different things because they can be enjoyed, even if it doesn't fit the way things have been for ages.

How about falling in love? Do we really fall, stumble, or get pushed into a loving, lasting and healthy relationship? I'm not throwing rocks at romance, as it can be a very affectionate, fun-filled emotional adventure, which touches our tender sense of feeling wanted and needed. But people who have tried to make that the foundation for a lasting friendship and marriage are among the 54% who are found in divorce court within ten years from the nuptials, disillusioned, discouraged, full of raw emotions and hatred because romance betrayed them.

We will explore two people who are examining themselves, with a heart full of love to share with someone else, build a lasting, healthy, productive relationship that will sustain them through their years. They still go on romantic dates, still find ways to show that they are special while the other reciprocates. There is mutual consideration, compassion, empathy (not sympathy), and a genuine sense of doing things just for the pure joy it gives the giver.

No one expects Mary, or Bill, who they met and made a commitment to, to suddenly turn out to be a total stranger. The expectation should be to grow up in the relationship and become a better version of who we are, but at the same time, not to fall into the trap of identity theft. In the beginning of the relationship, we have our given names. Endearing nick names creep in for summoning each other, then the children come along, turning names into mommy and daddy. For some, the evolution continues to grandpa and grandma. Those labels fit the current situation, but they don't define the person.

We are still Mary and Bill, and we still have goals, dreams, and desires in life, and we cannot afford to allow those to become diminished or forgotten. What happens if we do is they become lodged in our wishful mind and live there with an unspoken resentment because we traded them for the labels we wear. Using the tools provided here, you can have both. You might have the role of teacher or engineer, but you are deeper than the title. And when you are true to yourself, then no one can tell you that you are doing it wrong.

Chapter Four

Creating Goals Together

We are only as sick as our secrets. Honesty in this step is crucial. It will be counterproductive if you have anything in your heart that you can't share with your partner. Keeping it inside doesn't change the fact that it exists, and as long as it does, there is a part of you that isn't present in your life with your partner. To share something you've kept quiet doesn't create an obligation, but only opens a door for discussion. Often people find that the very thing they have kept secret was also something that their spouse was thinking about as well. By speaking about something that doesn't require immediate action, but rather careful planning to bring about something that will enrich the marriage.

After checking your inventory and making a list of your goals for your marriage, you will share them with each other. Upon sharing, you can make gestures, smile, or give a hug when the other is finished sharing. It is important though that no one is interrupted in any way.

This may be one of the rare chances anyone will have to give this much total focus to their goals. This, of course, is not the way it needs to be, but I'm a realist, and I know that once a few weeks or months have passed, we will see some type of relapse from this level of attention. People get busy in their lives and need interventions to help them remember the importance of putting first things first in their marriage. As you begin to write your list of goals, here are some questions and thoughts to consider.

A Vision of Self: Questions and Reflections for Self-Inventory and Evaluation

Regardless of the present image that you may hold of yourself, consider:

What is the truth about me?

- beyond my personality flaws and faults

- beyond my limited physical abilities

- beyond my mistakes

- beyond my limited intellectual abilities

I am the unique me that God created -- strong, capable, loving, confident, intelligent, joyous, and open to life!

I am a spiritual being in the eternal process of discovering all that god made me to be.

I am in a life that may appear to be tedious, intimidating, even hopeless. It may seem at times that the pain is not worth enduring, that life is too difficult, that I can't do this, or just plain baffling.

There is a life force within me that transcends all that, that is temporary, and has no permanent reality. Those things are that the process is about, but I am more than the process.

The mark of success is upon me! I hold firm to this truth because this is the truth of me. I am spirit's child, wonderfully made, and all that life needs to do can be done through me. I will succeed beyond all odds because the life force within me is greater than anything that could befall me.

With this vision of self and having shared that vision with a mate who sees themselves as the same, it is now likely that the goals set forth in the marriage will be met. It is also expected that both people will show the courage to make their own needs known to their partner.

In moving forward, we need to identify the major purposes, needs and goals in the marriage, as well as in the individuals who share this relationship. Survey the following questions and record your answers in your journals.

A. <u>Purposes:</u>
1. Why do I want to be married?
(personal motives)
2. What are the main purposes of our marriage?
(are they worth striving for?)
(do they inspire and energize the couple?)
B. <u>Goals:</u>
1. What are my individual needs and desires?
2. What are my married needs and desires?

Here are some elements to consider as you do your work. Some of these areas may already be receiving your attention and some may have been neglected.

Spiritual - praying, meditating, worshipping, studying about spiritual growth.

Mental - education, reading, activities to stimulate the mind.

Emotional - participating in, or appreciating music, arts, touching, loving, love making.

Physical/health - exercise, nutrition, rest

Family/children - needs, time for, activities, welfare

Social/recreational - entertaining, friendships, vacations, outdoors, hobbies, times to allow the inner child time to play

Material/financial - careers, home, income, investments, a plan to give.

As couples stimulate a conversation, new energy and direction comes to their marriage. For some, this is the first time they have ever had an exchange with this degree of intimacy. Couples do not start out a marriage with all the trust, wisdom, and insight they can develop later, particularly when they attend a seminar or retreat, or embark on activities to stimulate growth.

You will also find great advice in Love by Emmet Fox and Blessing for a Marriage by James Dillet Freeman. These will serve as reminders for couples of all the good that is possible for a marriage and what love in expression looks like.

At the conclusion of this part of the program you will be thinking about renewing your vows with what has been revealed by your work thus far. The setting for your new vows will be contingent on time, place, and opportunity, but the real focus is on a new agreement you two have made to live your lives. Anniversaries will be a progress check to see how well those newfound agreements are working, with no fear of making the needed changes. You won't get it perfectly right the first time. And as you continue to grow even more will be revealed.

Part Two:

Into Action to Love Me More

Chapter Five

Exercise: The Shameless Blameless Game

This game is designed to break the co-dependent shame and blame game, by reversing the way it's played. The broken, earlier version that has been beaten to death for centuries goes like this: one person must be 100% right, and the other person must be 100% wrong, and it takes two sick people to keep it going. If either or both begin to experience healthy thoughts, beliefs and behaviors, the game would be over.

In the original version, nothing ever gets resolved because no one takes responsibility for their own actions. This is predicated upon the adage: "he who smiles when things go wrong, has found someone else to blame it on."

The game goes on with bickering, blaming, and finger pointing and continues until someone refuses to play.

The new version of the shameless blameless game found in this chapter is played by each of you taking full responsibility for your feelings and actions, regardless of what prompted it. Just because someone does something that you find annoying doesn't make your reaction their fault. Your personal happiness, well-being, and good behavior do not depend on the other person. It is possible to voice feelings without attacking your partner's point of view. You can even agree to disagree with no loss of dignity or respect.

Follow the instructions, and once it's completed, the game continues to the next step. At this point, neither party is communicating directly with the other, each is completing his or her own list but not sharing it yet.

The basis for this game is to illustrate that you do influence each other, but no one can make anyone else feel or do anything.

1. Take a blank sheet of paper and draw a line down the center, and a line across the top to form a "t." One side of the t is labeled, "what my partner does" and the other side is labeled, "how I feel and what I do". Hint: thoughts and feelings do not have to have a realistic basis for existing. They need only to be a part of your belief and value system.

    ○ You will each complete your list to your satisfaction, and upon completion will fold the paper in half. Next, tear the paper down the center, vertical line. Keep the part that says, "how I feel and what I do" and throw away the side that says, "what my partner does".

2. With the remaining slip, you each have a list of your reactions that you can now take full responsibility for and begin to amend to sensible, sane, and loving behaviors, beliefs, and outcomes. A careful review will allow you to see how your normal upbringing and maturation has taught a set of standards. These are all defense mechanisms designed to protect fragile egos and give a false sense of righteousness.

3. This mini-inventory will now become part of the work that will follow. There will be two steps before you are finished with this list.

- A careful review will ensure, and during this time of contemplation, you will decide if there are any feelings, thoughts, or reactions you are ready to release. If you are in fact ready to release those old ways, they will now be written on a new piece of paper. When completed, both of you will silently place your list in a fire-safe bowl and set ablaze as a symbol that they are forgiven and that you purpose to forsake the behaviors on the list. A new list will be compiled which states what the new value/tool will be used in place of those discarded.

- For those items on the original list which you aren't ready to release, there is a place on one of the next exercises which will be discussed very soon. For now, though, you will prefix each item with this statement: "when this comes up, I feel...." The value of this is to recognize that it isn't what happens, but that you are responsible for what they do about it.

Summation – "My thoughts and feelings belong to me, and no one else has any responsibility for them; therefore, if they are causing me pain and I need to change them, I am now willing to admit I have them. The shameless and blameless game continues."

Fair fighting: Managing Conflict Effectively

When couples fight, it's because they don't feel their points can't be made, or that they can't win the argument without their point of view being passionately displayed, even at the expense of their mate. A lot of couples are still locked into the idea that in every argument, someone must win. The flaw of course in this line of thinking is that only one person can be a winner. The purpose of this session is to help couples take down their defensive barriers, and replace them with healthy, functional boundaries.

Each of you will have an opportunity after a brief presentation of the topic to respond to three questions: 1) how have you managed conflict with your mate thus far? 2) how do you feel about it? 3) how will you manage it in the future? The answers to the questions are to be from your point of view and is not intended to be a time of criticism, blame, or irresponsibility. Each of you will talk about your feelings, doubts, fears, successes, and failures in resolving conflict. Most people discover that this is not a skill that they have developed. Not only is this art lacking in marriage, but it is often a failure in all other inter- personal relationships.

Conflict occurs between any two or more people when they feel there is something everyone wants, but don't feel there is enough of the desired commodity to go around, or when their values, or agendas in life are very different, and this difference causes adversity. No two people hold the same opinion or values in all areas of life. It would be boring if they did. Conflict is natural, and very healthy, if people who experience it realize that their diversity can work for a more exciting, stimulating, and productive relationship for everyone.

This comparison describes two different ways to handle conflict and shows what the outcome of both methods is likely to produce. Consider both choices, and then decide which is most likely to give you the sense of freedom and genuine esteem.

Everyone Wins, Everyone Loses
Author Unknown
Everyone Loses

When one or both feels winning is the most important thing to do.

Conflict is seen as personal criticism: "I'm not okay."

Conflict is seen as a struggle for power and control.

Conflict generates fear, loss of love control, identity.

Refusal to cooperate.

One or both withdraw from conflict to process as a way to avoid feared consequences.

One member may use force, violence, or threats to silence another.

One or both brings in material from the past to prove something.

Loss of hope that things can or will ever change increases.

Self is valued more than the relationship.

Someone is to "blame" for the problem.

Mutual loss of respect and caring and self-esteem is lowered.

Members move further apart. Isolation increases.

Everyone Wins

When both people have a winning attitude from the outset
and the goal is to solve the issue.

Conflict is a normal part of living with someone else.

Conflict is seen as a signal that resolution is needed. It doesn't mean
anything is wrong.

Conflict is faced with confidence that both people are loved and important.

Both parties are to compromise

Steps will be taken toward resolution.

The couple agrees that force prolongs conflict.

Only the present problem is discussed. The past belongs to itself.

There is an enduring hope for future growth.

Solving the problem is more important than winning the argument.

Both members own the problem and become responsible for the joint solution.

Mutual respect and self-esteem grow with increased feeling of self-worth.

Members move closer as understanding increases.

The piece shows very clearly that assertive conflict will solve problems and enhance growth as couples share more maturity, honesty, and integrity with each other. This forum is set up so that blaming and shaming will not be a part of the experience.

The first item points out that winning is an attitude of growth, and not a score card that people keep on each other. Couples who keep score cards make it to where one feels like a loser, and the only way to feel a sense of self-esteem is to win the argument at any cost.

Conflict and attack are not synonymous, as a lot of people think. Conflict only shows that the status quo has been tampered with and not that anyone or anything is necessarily wrong.

Compromise means score keeping is removed. Compromise is a willingness to allow your partner to help you with something, which is what is really wanted anyway. The difference is that compromise doesn't care what the percentage is, it only wants to return to peace.

A person who feels they need to use force, or violence, or any form of manipulation is afraid of losing. The fact is, if violence is part of the scenario, that person does lose self-respect, and that of the partner. One basic flaw in our whole social system is the idea that one person can really make someone else do something they are not motivated to do. You may be able to coerce someone into temporary submission, but that will be short lived.

Bringing up past events only proves that the person who brought them up is still hurting, not that the other person is wrong. Once those hurts have been healed, they cease to be important to us. The fact is, if we can't solve the current problem, there isn't any point in bringing up the past either. Dredging up past events only cements the present situation in an attitude of hopelessness. If it has been this way forever, there is little likelihood that it will change with one more pointless argument. Couples need to look at their cumulative history, and it will be glaringly obvious.

If someone is to blame in the argument, that means someone has come away with less esteem, respect, or dignity, and the problem is still not going to get solved. This creates the feeling of isolation, and forces people apart. Use of "you are" messages point the finger of guilt and shame, and rather than getting rid of responsibility for each person's part in the problem, it only grows, and both people then feel depleted and helpless. It appears the problem has done something to the marriage, but it's really the unwillingness of one or both people that allows it to go to the point that it consumes the relationship.

Your discussion during this step, centered around the foregoing, will ensure everyone has a good working knowledge of what conflict is, what it means in marriage, and what can be carried out when people have the courage to face life honestly and together. The problem belongs to the relationship. We do not live our lives in a vacuum. This will certainly give couples good cause for the divorce court, which is coming up next.

Setting the Stage for a Fair Fight
With Two Winners

There should be a venue set up that will foster a fair fight. Conflict and the resolution of it is essential in a healthy relationship. It is not if it occurs, but when it occurs. Couples are wise to set some healthy boundaries and agreements as to how to proceed so the fight remains fair and profitable. In extreme cases in working with couples over the years, on a few occasions I have resorted to suggesting that when they decide a fight is brewing, that they both get naked, get down on their hands and knees, and get to fighting! There's a much simpler and less drastic way to go about it, but if all else fails, give it a try.

Pick a peaceful time when there are no major conflicts on the table, and sit down and write out an agreement that sets the following boundaries:

1. Each person will call the other by their first name, and no character assassination is allowed. Each person deserves mutual respect, and the best way to ensure this is to share your self-respect with your partner.

2. Listen to each other. Use an object such as a checker, stuffed toy, or large coin, to be held by the person whose turn it is to speak with the other person only listening. Some may find it helpful to keep their remarks to five minutes or less. If you can't state your

point at that time, you are not prepared to enter this discussion. An egg timer can be used if necessary.

3. Volume control-speak no louder than necessary for someone in the same room as you to be heard. When you yell, the other person stops listening.

4. Dignity-no put-downs; either self-inflicted (a grasp for pity) or casting any dispersion on the other person, remember, this is the one you picked.

5. "I" messages-it is perfectly well and needed, that you articulate your feelings, while remembering that they belong to you, and by doing so allows your partner to understand what you're going through, and can have compassion for you as long as it isn't an attack on them. Example: "when we're late sitting down to dinner, I feel frustrated, as I spent a lot of time preparing the meal and I'm hungry and ready to eat".

6. We feel-this is a statement that two parents with a united front will use when discussing something with one of the children. This is one of the major stumbling blocks in parenting, as we were all raised differently, and have developed some unhealthy practices with the children for reasons of convenience, and/or fear they are going to be side wiped or ignored. Triangulation occurs when parents differ on their styles and beliefs and don't have these worked out and attempt to do one arm ruling, and the children unfortunately love nothing better than to get in between you and bang your heads together.

7. Stick to the issue-it is unfair and unproductive to use the kitchen sink method when something is brought up. When someone decides to add on other issues which are unrelated to the one at hand, it is because these have either not been discussed, or were not resolved when they were. One thing a couple can do is set a limit on the number of times and a time frame in which an issue can be brought up or rehashed. If the limit is exceeded, they agree to make an appointment with a marriage counselor and work out the issue with an unemotional third party. Healthy people get counseling, while sick people end up in therapy.

8. Time outs-time outs are allowed and should be used when either or both are over tired, at the boiling point, or just need a few minutes to collect their thoughts. Time outs shouldn't last more than a few minutes or much of the value of the session is diminished. If either or both decide not to continue at this time, it can be put on the calendar at a date which matches the urgency of the issue. Nothing works better here than common sense and mutual respect.

The Ten Demandments

Ten rules to live by to ensure unhappiness in a relationship:

I. Thou shalt make me happy.

II. Thou shalt not have any interests other than me.

III. Thou shalt know what I feel without me having to say.

IV. Thou shalt return each one of my sacrifices with an equal or greater sacrifice.

VI. Thou shalt give me my sense of self-worth and esteem.

VII. Thou shalt be grateful for everything I do.

VIII. Thou shalt not be critical of me, show anger toward me, or otherwise disapprove of anything I do.

IX. Thou shalt be so caring and loving that I never need to risk or be vulnerable in any way.

X. Thou shalt love me with thy whole heart, thy whole soul, and they whole mind, even when I do not love myself.

Chapter Six

Exercise: Divorce Court

I f you don't like your marriage the way it is, get a divorce! Yes, that's my advice to couples who claim they are unhappy with their version of wedded bliss. But rather than sending them to get a lawyer, go to court, cut up the bank accounts, the kids, the property, and the visitation rights, I encourage them to get another type of divorce. It's called the No-Blame Divorce. In this type of proceeding, rather than make allegations against the partner in the marriage, each spouse takes responsibility for his or her own unhappiness by filing a petition of honest acceptance for their own part of the state of the marriage.

The stipulation clause of the divorce decree says that nothing happens in a vacuum in marriage. Each partner has allowed their own lack of courage, clarity of vision, failure to speak their minds, express their feelings, or make their needs known, and this has created emotional and spiritual distancing. Marriage is an integrated experience, and whatever one person does or does not do, has some effect on their partner. The partner is not responsible for what the other spouse does, but they are responsible for how they act upon, or react to what is happening. This happens most often when couples try to run their lives on limited emotional energy, and there is a lack of daily prayer. We become mechanical in our movement through life, and boredom and confusion about why happiness seems to be so elusive becomes part of the conversation. Perhaps there is no conversation. Some couples just make assumptions that their partner either doesn't understand, doesn't care or doesn't want to care. They do not check this out with their spouse, so their partner sits there wondering the same thing. Whether or not this becomes a dysfunctional marriage depends on what the couples do about it.

Rather than physical separation, which is usually what occurs in a divorce, we are instead creating emotional separation. We remove both people from the midst of the turmoil and have them separate their own feelings from that of their spouse. In this way, we can begin to establish objectivity. There does not have to be any major problem in the marriage for this exercise to be helpful. Healthy couples at regular intervals will step back and look at how enmeshed they have become, and take a mature, and sensible approach to redefining their own personal boundaries. This does not cause separation, rather it allows more intimacy.

During the separation, before the actual petitions are filed, each partner will prepare their own suit. The following format will be used. Since this separation is going to end in divorce, I need to clarify that the marriage is not ending, but in this exercise, you are terminating the habits, attitudes, behaviors, and beliefs that have kept this spiritual union from being all that it can be.

Each case will be tried in an open court (both people are present, and everything said will honest and forthright) and the couple will be the judge of how they feel about amending their marriage contract with each other. Each will be given their "day in court" to testify to their own needs, goals, dreams, and willingness to make a renewed commitment to themselves that will be shared with their partner. There is no judgment but rather discernment and mutual consideration of the possibilities for growth and happiness. The "judgment of the court" is the total acceptance by both parties to apply a new approach to the issues.

***

In this step, each of you will create a written petition, not revealing it to your partner. Since the respondent is not going to be accused of anything, there is no need for prior disclosure.

Each of you will create your own petition. You can copy the following template onto a handwritten petition or type a document for printing. Add your names, dates, lists, and other items where indicated.

In the circuit court of the conscious awareness of both people, in the marriage of _____ and _____,

Note: Do not serve; participants will respond at the court hearing
<u>Petition for dissolution of old habits, beliefs,</u> and hindrances in the above stated marriage

Comes now participant, under oath, and for participant's cause of action needed to restore this marriage to its fullest potential and level of happiness and success, states and alleges that:

1. Participant has been willfully involved in this marriage for <u>state length of marriage</u>, consummated on <u>anniversary date,</u> prior to the commencement of this action.

2. Participant is an adult, but has a child within, still growing and continuing to express the love of God the creator and seeks by this action to increase this expression to a greater extent than before

known.

3. Participant has learned, because of the preceding separation, that the following old habits, angers, misconceptions, lies, and/or other resistance to life, have resulted in a need to release custody of said items as they are listed in this petition in paragraph 4.

4. Participant accepts ownership of the following and prays that the presence of God in this court action will grant relief, in the form of forgiveness from their pain and misery: in this space, list your selfish, self- centered, habits, attitudes, sense of failure, or anything else you discover standing in the way of you being the marriage partner of your shared vision. (here is where the list from the shameless blameless game is inserted) This gives each person an opportunity in a safe, understanding environment to confront some old fears, or new ones, and share with their partner in a productive, loving, non-threatening way.

5. There remains no reason why this marriage should continue from this day as it has in the past. It is now declared and affirmed that improvement on the very best can only bring further success and joy to this partnership.

Wherefore, participant prays for the relief from the form of this marriage in its present state by making a commitment to the following new guidelines: in this space, write your renewed commitment to a healthier marriage, and what you will do to ensure that commitment will be kept. This, of course, has not been shown to your marriage partner at this point.

Finding that there is no further desire to continue living in the past, prays for the dissolution of the faults in this marriage.

It is further judged that the participant is hereby ordered from within to hold self-harmless from the mistakes or seeming mistakes of the past and can now go forth into the new marriage contract. All shame, malice, or self-hatred is hereby set aside.

For such just and proper adjustments to this union, as it is attuned to the spiritual laws of the universe, this harmonious resolution is hereby entered on <u>today's date.</u>

***

As each person completes their decree, they will enter their pleas in the court of marital consciousness. Each will in turn share with the other what they have written, and after each has shared, will make an affirmation of acceptance of their partner's new commitment to the marriage.

The divorce decrees will be kept together after the court recesses, so that couples will have a reminder of what they agreed to do. Of course, writing it down and sharing it is only the beginning of a time of growth that is yet to come. Couples discover in this process that a lot of what they need a divorce from did not come from the marriage, but from the lives they lived before meeting their spouse. Couples are encouraged to hold a "divorce court" each year before celebrating their anniversary, or as part of the anniversary celebration. This is not to throw any negative energy into anniversaries, but to amplify the strengths in the marriage by celebrating the overcoming of old ideas. At this time, each person can look at where they are in their ability to share their best and make a concerted effort to improve in the coming year.

The value in sharing all the divorces at one time is for people to see that most people have the same personal ills. This can be a very supportive, productive, and fun way for each person to do the self-observation needed to keep their marriage working, or to get un-stuck if in fact that is the case. This is the way to achieve and preserve true intimacy and a real heart connection.

Place the petitions together in a labeled envelope to be stored in a private, accessible compartment.

Chapter Seven

Exercise: The Relationship Resume

Before getting into the relationship resume, I need to tell you this is not a textbook idea. When my wife and I decided to consider another marriage, and we'd both struck out a couple of times, I had just written these exercises and asked her if she would be willing to do them with me. That was 34 years ago, and while it may not have been the only secret to our success, it kept us from making a lot of our old mistakes. It was around that time that I began a 15-year stretch of teaching marriage classes in the family court system.

When going through this process, I recommend focusing on the key spiritual principles of restoration, integrity, personal value, authenticity, vulnerability, purpose, trust, being true to yourself, humility, and sharing openly.

Instructions for Relationship Resume and Boundary Circles

This exercise is designed to name and commit to using spiritual principles to support a healthy relationship. This can be used for any type of personal bonding with another person, or even in an organization, team, or any other way we wish to relate to someone else. The primary platform is simple: if we choose principles instead of personalities as the basis for forming a relationship, it will be well-founded, and even if the relationship isn't the fulfillment one is seeking, it can still end up with a meaningful and lasting form. Principles before personalities simply means that marriage honors truth above the personalities that make up the relationship. Principles are Godlike guides to living that are not swayed by emotion or human traits which are changeable. Principles are always true and don't vary by conditions. Love, tolerance, perseverance, compassion, respect, and loyalty are just some of them.

The very first question relates to your expectations of what you will receive in return for your investment in this relationship. Expectations do not relate to the other person, only that it reminds you of what you value.

1. **What do I expect to receive in my life from my relationship?** Perhaps your answer is honesty, integrity, growth, and personal sense of fulfillment. Perhaps you want to relate to someone who can share your common core values and has the honesty and willingness to share and appreciate the differences. Maybe you expect to be supportive of your spouse and receive likewise. It's important that your answer is honest and true to you.

2. **What attributes/qualities do I need from the person in my relationship?** This question relates to what you are looking for in attributes from the other person. This is not about changing them to suit you when you meet someone who simply doesn't have the same spiritual equivalents. In addition to the physical and social characteristics of an individual, do you need someone who holds the same spiritual values? Obviously, things like honesty and integrity are the standard requirements but it's important to recognize things like compassion, humility, and those qualities we don't think enough about. This list needs to be very comprehen-

sive.

3. **Next, place a star (*) next to the items above that you are willing to negotiate.** After looking over those qualities in the above question, you now must discern which, if any, are things you can be swayed on, that would be nice to have, but aren't deal killers. The purpose of this question is to decide how rigid and rigorously honest you are being with yourself. The catch here is that a healthy relationship consists of two whole people who aren't looking for someone else to fill up their holes. You must be willing to share the same level of spiritual value with the other person that you expect of them. If you are puzzled about your answers, you probably have some work to do in discernment. Trusting yourself is simply your ability and willingness to rely on your intuitive resources.

4. **What are the best qualities you bring into the relationship?** Expounding on your virtues is not an ego trip, but rather to recognize your identity and strengths, and whether you're willing to share them with your partner without any need for approval or recognition. Be detailed when making this list.

5. **What qualities in you are still "under construction"?** This is the freedom zone. Here is where you declare, "I am not perfect." Neither partner should have to play the "walking on eggshells" game where you find out about each other's flaws. Making this list, you will be very open about the things you are aware of in your spiritual development. Here are three things that this needs to communicate to your partner: 1. You didn't cause this, as I did

when I met you. 2. I only need your ongoing support; you don't need you to fix me. 3. I don't expect you to be perfect either, so we can drop the games and be open to sharing our inner child without worrying about them getting beaten up.

6. **Next, list what you are willing to commit to in the relationship.** The answers to this question go on the following diagram with the 3 circles, which are dated today, 3 months from now, and 6 or 9 months from now (you can set the dates you both agree on. Everything you list here goes inside the circle).

7. **List what you are unwilling to commit to in this relationship**. The answers to this question go on the outside of the circle until the next review date and may be moved or may stay inside or outside the circle.

   ○ Note: the circles stand for boundaries. Boundaries are what keep the environment healthy, and you will be responsible for everything inside. You are not responsible for what goes on outside the boundary.

Note: this inventory is to be kept in a sealed envelope and opened for your review and amazement in _____ weeks/months.

Three circles for setting healthy boundaries in relationships

For each interval, Today, 3 Months, 6 Months, everything that you are willing to commit to, #6, goes inside the square.

Everything you are unwilling to commit to, #7, goes outside the circle. Then place the sheet inside the envelope and date for the upcoming review and then open it and make adjustments.

Today

3 Months

6 Months

Copyright Doc Golden 2001

Part Three:

Into the Future of Loving You Better

Chapter Eight

Exercise: The Dating Game

D on't let this scare you. Who wants to think of getting on a dating app when you are well out of your teens? No one really, but since you already have that person with you, half the battle is already won, or at least so it seems.

Now that the divorce is concluded, it's time to get on with the business of dating again. There are many variations of dating games on television, most of which have to do with blind dating. That is the people don't know each other before the date. I've decided to take this concept a little further. The couples who are going on their first date will be those who have finally divorced themselves from all the things they have discovered were holding them back in their marriage. They are now ready to experience each other in a new and different way. On Love Connection, a dating game that aired on television in the eighties and nineties, the couples planned their date, and tell the experiences they had on their blind date. In the love better edition in this chapter, you will have your date planned for you, and you will then discuss how you experience the date and the difference in your experience from earlier dates together.

The date will not be blind, but silent. You will use the script and itinerary given here, but the primary focus of this date is to engage the spiritual essence of each other silently in the presence of God, rather than be concerned about where you will go, and what you will eat, and so forth.

This timed date will last about 45 minutes. A timer can be used so you don't have to look at your watch the whole time. The venue for this exercise can be any outdoor setting which allows the couple to be apart from anyone else and the regular noises. Any emergency that may develop will of course put safety first. There are many walking trails, lake sides, and nature centers where couples can find the solace and peace needed.

Keep this affirming prayer with you throughout the date to recite when instructed.

You and Me and God Together

"God, we want you walking closely with us, as we travel the path of life together."

The following walk will be taken in silence, so you can realize that there is no aloneness. Walk together for about 50 yards and stop. Look around you.

Notice what is far away, and what is close to you.

Look up at the sky and then back down to the earth you are standing on.

Take note of things at an intermediate distance.

What are you feeling?

Where do you see yourself in this picture?

Where do you see your partner?

What impresses you most about the surroundings?

Before continuing, stop and silently affirm together:

"Thank you, Spirit God, for surrounding us with your presence".

Make a non-verbal decision to walk in a direction that feels good for both.

Note: it will soon become clear that this is not an activity couples will want to give a lot of energy to. It is here where both people realize that something special is going to happen to both of them, no matter which way they go. They will allow the gentleness of spirit to direct them. If they go one way at this time, and find one thing, they can decide to go another direction later, and see what that experience is like, but it will not be an "all or nothing" choice. It's valuable for people to realize that it isn't where you go, but what happens to you along the path really matters. Here is where couples can put to work some new ideas they have perceived from previous hours of this experience. A man who usually wants to be the leader, may be willing to allow his partner to take the reins. A woman who generally followed her husband's lead, may want to initiate the new direction taken. This is a safe arena for risk taking. The will of individual personality will give way to the guidance of God.

For the first 15 minutes, walk side by side, but not making any contact, just sharing the space on the path, just taking in your surroundings, and occasionally pointing out anything you see that sparks your interest. It might be a tree, an animal, or a stone. Stop momentarily and notice it, pay attention to give your mate your attention when they notice something. For the next 15 minutes, hold hands or put your arms around each other's waist, so that you feel more connected as you continue to walk along. Stop and look into each other's eyes, give a hug or kiss, feel the texture of each other's hands, and then continue to walk,

While you walk, feel the earth beneath your feet. What is its texture? Is it easy to walk on? What effect does the weather have on you? Is the sun warm on your skin? Are you aware of the unseen air that surrounds you? Breathe deeply. Sense the air passing through your body.

Before continuing the walk, silently affirm together: "God, we feel what we cannot see. Your presence is real". Walk quickly for 50 feet. Pause for a moment and jog for 50 feet. Pause again, and rest. When you are ready, move forward as if you are a leaf driven by the wind. For example, turn, bend, stop, start, move your arms around you and above your head. Be the leaf and sense the strength and support of spirit. Discover God's plan for you.

This exercise exemplifies that the pace of life changes. They may each choose to bend, stop, or start at different times, or in different ways, but they can still share all that life gives, and remain together in God's grace and peace. This is a very releasing feeling. I often find that men enjoy the permission to allow their body to move in ways that are not usually considered manly. Women enjoy the courage of their partner and appreciate being joined as they allow themselves to flow with life without feeling they will leave their partner behind. Each person will have their journal with them to record anything they wish. Rest from your turning and moving, but let your mind be compelled by what you cannot see. Without breaking the flow observe and record any thoughts or feelings that are important.

Before continuing along the path, silently affirm together: "God's wisdom and intelligence directs us on the path to our good".

As you allow the guidance to direct your steps, on this walk you will find an object which will have a spiritual meaning to you. When you discover your object, carry it with you for the rest of the walk. You will have an opportunity to share it with your partner later. This is a very important aspect of this journey. Each will have his/her own special gift that will become apparent to them, and it can be just for them. While we share the joy, and the peace, and the growth of being married, we also need to share the freedom for our mate to find some special experience that is theirs alone. One of the things that I enjoy about my marriage is that I can buy my wife something without her feeling like she has to reciprocate, just because she got something.

The last time I went on a walk like this, I found something that became very special to me, and I found it in a very unusual place. Although it's somewhat crumpled, I am going to include it here because it provided a breakthrough for me. I was feeling very stressed during this peaceful experience, because it was almost time for the walk to be completed, and I had not found my object yet. I was wandering (aimlessly I thought) around the grounds of a retreat center and found myself rooting around in a wood pile next to an outdoor grill. There was a tinder box full of small pieces of kindling, and paper. I started wondering what I was doing, then I came across the picture of the little girl looking up at the huge strawberries in the upper corner of the picture. As I looked at the picture, I began to write a poem on a blank check I found in my wallet. The poem was shared with a group I was with, as was the picture.

The child

I am a child, so small,

The universe so big, so tall.

How can I matter, look at my size,

Can from my small gift, something great realize?

Then everywhere I look, I begin to see,

God's miracles all matter, even ones as small as me.

I realized that although I felt very insignificant in relationship to the size of the universe, my life really counted for a lot. I have known this for certain, but it's easy to forget when you are caught up in the competitive world we live in. On your walk you could find anything. Some pick flowers, or find a leaf, or some other natural object. My picture represented important aspects of life. I'm not sure what the photographer was trying to capture with the camera, but it was a very meaningful message for me.

As you continue walk, let your powers of observation make you aware of the many sounds around you. Listen to the sounds of your walking. Stop, listen to the sounds your walking has masked, and then walk again. Pause again, and listen for the wind, or faint sounds in the distance. Which sounds originated from nearby and which have distant sources? What sounds are pleasant and add to your sense of peace? Are there sounds which you find disturbing?

This part of the exercise points to how much outer clatter reduces or drowns out the inner voice of peace and wisdom. It also helps couples compare what is pleasing to each of them, and what they find uncomfortable. When communicated at that level, people tend to have a higher regard for what the other person needs or wants and see it as diversity instead of an adversity. It doesn't mean that anything is wrong, just that we all have our personal preferences for what we like. If both people honor each other, the real voice of spirit will be heard.

Before continuing on the path together, stop and silently affirm "wonderful and loving God, we are open and receptive to your still small voice as it speaks to us from within".

Continue walking, but as you do, look for a place where you can sit and be still for a time. Let yourself be drawn to a place by the other partner who did not pick the first direction you took. As you come to rest, allow your senses to become attuned to all that surrounds you. Silently describe your surroundings. Do they relate to the universe within yourself? What are your current thoughts? Jot them down. What are you feeling right now? Have your feelings or   thoughts changed since the beginning of your date? If so, how? Have you found your object yet? This segment re-enforces thinking vs. feeling. It also emphasizes the fact that when we become still and put ourselves in perspective to the rest of the universe, our troubles don't seem so big, and our opinions don't seem to matter so much. Silently affirm together "loving God, we find you in the stillness and rest, as we leave our worldly troubles behind us, there you are".

When you feel guided, rise, and proceed at a leisurely pace. Amble rather than walk and become sensitive to any fragrances in the air. Walk to the nearest plant and become aware of its fragrance. If it feels good, hold it in your hand and feel its texture. Before continuing, silently affirm the following: "we feel the life of God in all that we touch".

Note: it's interesting how many people will want to pick a flower, while others will want to let it continue to grow, and just enjoy it without needing to remove it from the earth. This says something about personal habits that before probably went unnoticed.

Now, begin to return to the place where this date originated, and speak to no one as you walk, and pause to touch and smell.

As many things as you can. Touch the grass. Walk barefoot if you like. Is the grass warm or cool to your touch? Hug a tree on your return. Hug a person on your return.

Let love empower you. God is with you, and ever constant companion, a part of everything, and everyone. As you return to the beginning, notice the new vision you have of yourself, and your partner. You get a glimpse of true intimacy and experience the true love of God in your marriage.

Enter the room where you began, silently praying:

"Thank you, God, for chaperoning our date".

As the couple enters the room where they began, they should remain silent and prepare for the next stage and use the instructions that follow.

You will need paper, markers, scissors, pencils, and pens.

Using these materials and anything you found on your date, express what this experience has meant to you, or what you discovered about yourself and/or your partner. You may want to write a letter, a poem, or draw a picture of that which describes your experience, or you may write a narrative.

After this is completed, each of you will turn to your partner to share your expression and explain its meaning.

The one important factor in sharing is that while a person is talking about their experience, no one is allowed to interrupt. There is so much feeling and expression that comes out when couples give each other the time and space and listening ear. Couples will be encouraged to go on a silent date often and realize how important the experiences are that they have together. Dinner will be by candlelight, with a very romantic conversation.

Chapter Nine

Exercise: The Remarriage Ceremony

If it interests you, one recommendation is to conduct this exercise at a chapel or wedding venue. This service will be the final part of this experience. This is something you can opt to do as a formal renewal of vows, using your minister or spiritual leader, or you may decide to script your own intimate experience with just the two of you present.

Prepare a unity candle placed in the center of a table, with two individual tapers on each side. The tapers will be lit at the beginning of the service, and the unity candle will be lit at a particular time later in the ceremony. The table can be prepared with a white linen tablecloth and arranged with flowers. Choose the music and prepare it ahead of time, if proper.

Weather allowing, this can be conducted outside. If the wind is a problem for the candles, hurricane lamps can be used to prevent this.

The service will begin with a processional. The couple will join at the rear of the chapel, room, or outdoor space and continue to the front and stand in front of the minister or ceremony leader. If the couple is performing their renewal of vows alone, they will already have all they want to say scripted. They may decide to have recorded music playing.

The minister (or couple) after the processional is complete, will open with a prayer: we give thanks that this couple (we) have come to this place in their/our lives. This is a time to re-affirm and recommit the vows and purpose of marriage. It is another opportunity to acknowledge the presence, power, love, and peace of spirit working its wonders through the partnership of marriage. Our hearts know this time as both joyful and sacred. We pray knowing that this truth will follow in the days ahead for these children of spirit, and we are truly grateful, amen.

Minister: "We are here today because this couple has chosen to share their path of life some time ago, and are choosing to continue to share the joys, rewards, and growth of life together. So, we are celebrating a renewal of vows."

Next, light unity candle and you or the minister will recite the following:

"Before us stand two burning candles. They symbolize the light of the living Christ that burns within each of you. The light that makes you a best friend to one another. Even though you have all grown in your expression of the love within you, you have also kept that unique spark of divine light that is yours alone to share. Your goals, dreams and ideals are still reflected in each other, and your recommitment here today will kindle new dreams, greater goals, and higher ideals. As you continue to grow together, remember to thine own self be true, for in this way you will always add to that which your partner shares, and nothing will be consumed or diminished."

Continue aloud with:

"The prophesy of marriage:
Kahlil Gibran spoke of the idea of marriage as such:
Love one another but make not a bond of love.

Let it be rather a moving sea between the shores of your souls. Fill each other's cup, but drink not from the same cup. Give one another your bread but eat not from the same loaf. Sing and dance together and be joyous, but let each of you be alone, even as the strings of a lute are alone, they quiver with the same music. Give your hearts, but not into each other's keeping. Only the hand of life can have your heart. And stand together, yet not too near together: for the pillars of the temple stand apart, and the oak tree and the cypress grow not in each other's shadow."

Continue aloud if your minister is conducting the ceremony:

"And now, would each of you in turn, take a candle from its place, and hold the flames together as you light the large single candle which symbolizes the oneness that is your marriage. As you put the candle back in their place, notice that the light still burns. That flame of love will be there to rekindle and renew you always."

Vows:

"_____ and _____, you each wrote a new covenant. Now, will you share those with each other? After this, the minister will instruct the couple to affirm "I will" in unison. Next, the minister will direct these questions to each of you: do you vow to keep one another as your loving companion, your strength in time of weakness, to share your dreams, desires, your love?

Will you cherish, protect, and provide for one another's needs as best you can. Will you be all to this marriage that you are able to be, if so, say "I will."

The couple will look at their mates, and together say, "I will".

Next recite this prayer together or have your minister pray:

"Wonderful, loving, and ever-present God, each member of this couple has spoken their vows to re-dedicate and consecrate their oneness with you in the partnership of their marriage. As they go forth into the joyful noise of life, we know they do so with your blessings. The prospering power of your love and presence here today, and in the days ahead, is the surety we have for growth and success in the days to come. For as you continue each year's celebration of this day, I invite you to relight this single candle as you did here today, and share with each other a blessing, such as the one I will share with you now."

God love you and keep you,
Blessing your going out and
Coming in.
May you walk in light, and your
Steps be as singing.
May you rejoice in your work,
And know the sweetness of duty
Performed in freedom.
May your hands be gentle in
Holding and tender in letting
Go.
May love illuminate your face,
And your kiss brings peace.
With the taking of vows, and
Through the power vested in me
By the Holy Spirit God which

Performs each true marriage,
I affirm that you are husbands
And wives, partners in marriage
Who go forth to live and move
And have your being in the
Oneness of God's eternal love.
You may seal your vows.
Benediction: may your growth
Be ever together, your dreams
Never far apart, and your love
Shared freely between you.
Richest blessings to you
in your future lives
Together.

You may decide to re-design this ceremony in a more simplistic way, or go through it as it is written, but however it is celebrated, it is the completion of this journey together through the pages of this book, and hopefully you will keep your written work handy to refer to often. The process of continued growth is just that, a never-ending journey through the love of life together.

Chapter Ten

For As Long as We Both Shall Live

Having taken the challenge and the time to go through this work, and by reflecting on the needed changes, you have made great strides toward renewing, healing, and strengthening your marriage and life. This is but a beginning because the old values, habits, beliefs, and behaviors have been with you for a long time. Now you have a new plan and a fresh look at the amazing treasures awaiting you, and you have the luxury of having a caring, understanding, and willing partner to continue to grow in joy and peace. Your new anniversary will be a good time to stop and review your progress, but if something comes up on the horizon beforehand, you needn't wait, but get right into whatever the issue(s) is and begin to work on it with your newfound practices, principles, and knowledge. What a relief it is to know that there is nothing you can't talk about and work out together to leave everyone happier and healthier. Keep your exercises close by and review them often until you sense them at an intuitive level. Don't overlook the value of seeing a counselor if you are in a situation you can seem to resolve. Healthy people see counselors, people go to a therapist for ill health. Neither of you should expect yourself nor your partner to always say and do the right thing. This book doesn't make you an expert nor render you white as snow. The more you celebrate your success (catching the other person getting it right), the more you will want to continue to use this pattern of living as your "go to" method for success.

Reflections and Strategies for the Development of a Healthy Marriage

It's important to cultivate a love affair. You cannot share the love of spirit with another person until you have had the experience within your own heart. When the love of God overflows you, it will be available in your life to share with another who has experienced the same outpouring.

Prioritize growing a friendship with your partner. Respecting yourself and each other, having fun together, and communicating freely at all stages of life is invaluable. When best friends get married, they stay friends, and no matter what happens during their lifetime together, they will remain friends as long as they administer continual care.

Don't neglect romance. This is the human side of love. In a healthy perspective, this fantastic "dream-like" stage can be a continuing part of your life, no matter how long you are together, as long as romance is not the purpose for being together. While it is one of the neat feelings you share, it by itself will not sustain a long-term commitment, nor can this emotional fervor take up too much time in your life. It is, however, a beautiful part of the human experience, and shouldn't be denied. A romantic interlude can help you remember some of the special magic that brought you together.

Commitment is vital. The decision to share the bounty of God's good with your spouse takes courage, persistence, strength, and vision. Commitment should be commensurate with the level of personal trust and willingness you share, and not overstate it for the sake of consummating the relationship. When you are secure in your faith, you won't choose a mate out of fear of losing them.

Keep in the spirit of negotiation. You share gifts that are brought to the relationship, hinderances to growth, and rules. Mature couples will find this confrontation period positive and productive. Insecure people will see it as threatening. This process will continue to present itself through the stages of growth of your relationship.

Practice genuine disclosure with each other. Build a relationship that enables each of you to share who you are because you're not afraid of being rejected. Each of you need to be able to share your most inward self that you have worked so hard to accept. In taking responsibility for your strengths, you must also take responsibility for your shortcomings. This requires a lot of courage and a safe zone between you and your partner. Marriage should be a no-shame place in the world.

Choose to live in resolution and acceptance. At each level of commitment, you agree to accept the issues that have been resolved. Together you can see that another part of growth has been completed and agree to enter the next level of your experience with courage and anticipation. There is peace at all levels. It just becomes more apparent as the relationship matures.

Act out in a way that makes love tangible. Purpose to engage in daily expressions of inspiring each other to live in full potential, and to share all that goes with it. Prioritize doing creative, loving, useful, and fun things together, acknowledging God in one another. Strive to make the expression of love plain in all that is done outwardly. Face each day with shared joy, success, and wish each other well in all that is undertaken. Unselfish support and encouragement are bound to the happiness of each of you discovering your divinity.

Communication and Understanding

Lastly, experts over the years have suggested learning how to interpret the "foreign languages" spoken by the opposite sex. When you learn to understand what your mate is trying to get across to you, feelings will be shared, needs will be met, and a lot of the guess work will be taken out of the marriage.

The following is based on ideas from two books: He Says, She Says by Lillian Glass (Glass, Lillian, *He Says, She Says*, Perigee Trade, 1993) and Men are From Mars, Women are From Venus, by John Gray (Gray, John, *Men are From Mars, Women Are from Venus*, Harper, 1993). The premise is that men and women simply don't speak the same language. A very interesting conversation between the royal couple in 1981 demonstrated this aptly. When Diana phoned Charles, her then fiancé, and said, "I really miss you darling", during his visit to New Zealand. His reply was, "Yes, I know". It doesn't take a heavy-duty imagination to figure out why they might be having difficulties in their marriage at this time. Their plight, unfortunately, is all too typical of many couples. I have found in working with professionals couples especially, and those where one family member works extended hours, communication is more than strained. In many instances a lack of real face to face time to discuss important issues, causes more problems than alcoholism and/or other drug addiction. When the problem becomes normalized it escapes the attention of both partners and serious consequences will occur, even up to divorce.

When couples arrive at home, the children are picked up from the day care, the TV is on, and the mechanical routine is re-enacted, there is little time and attention talking. When any conversation occurs, it may be misunderstood and never resolved. Some couples even drop to the level of only writing notes. This pattern continues into other areas such as sexual activity. Women enjoy the talk of foreplay, while men tend to prefer the physical contact. Without the talk, there probably won't be a lot of sexual contact. Women talk about their feelings as soon as they experience them, while men prefer to work through feelings before discussing them. Women will often talk of problems which have no solution, and men don't usually enjoy that type of conversation. The differences could be primarily due to how differently men and women are socialized. Women learn to ask questions to draw a man out in a conversation. Men, on the other hand, are more interested in solving problems, and getting at the facts, and see communication as a way to an end, rather than an objective in itself. The biggest disappointment in communications is when one person expects their mate to know what the other wants or needs.

The form What Planet are You from Anyway? Found in Men are from Mars, Women are from Venus can be a useful tool. He maintains that men and women are from two different parts of the solar system, and this is why an indirect request for help by the woman is seen as nagging by the men. The women will be given sample translations of what men mean, and the men will receive some clarity on what their partners mean. The hope is that when each is exposed to the other's form of communication, there will be a greater understanding of both parts.

Couples will begin to see why they find so much frustration with their mate and can't really put a finger on the problem. Coming to an understanding that there is a difference in the way they communicate, men and women can find peace in their diversity, and learn to allow their differences to be complimentary, rather than a grumbling standoff.

Couples are encouraged to utilize their newfound skills when talking to their partner.

Some people will agree with the materials, and others will not. The important thing is not whether the couples agree with all the material or not, but that they come to a mutual understanding of what they mean to each other. They need to discover what parts they have been doing well, and what things they agree need improvement. The important attitude about this discourse is that no one is wrong just because they have different opinions. This isn't about right or wrong; it's about what works and what doesn't.

Having taken the challenge and the time to go through this work, and by reflecting on the needed changes, you have made great strides toward renewing, healing, and strengthening your marriage and life. This is but a beginning because the old values, habits, beliefs, and behaviors have been with you for a long time. Now you have a new plan and a fresh look at the amazing treasures awaiting you. And you have the luxury of having a caring, understanding, and willing partner to continue to grow in joy and peace. Your new anniversary will be a good time to stop and review your progress, but if something comes up on the horizon beforehand, you needn't wait, but get right into whatever the issue(s) is and begin to work on it with your newfound principles and knowledge. What a relief it is to know that there is nothing you can't talk about and work out together in a way that leaves everyone happier and healthier. Keep your exercises close by and review them often until you sense them at an intuitive level. Don't overlook the value of seeing a counselor if you are into something you can seem to settle on. Healthy people see counselors, people go to a therapist for ill health. It should never be expected that you nor your partner always say and do the right thing. This book doesn't make you an expert nor render you white as snow. The more you celebrate your success; (catching your partner getting it right), the more you will want to continue to use this pattern of living as your "go to" method for success.

About the author

Rev. Dr. Ed "Doc" Golden is a minister, psychologist, author, and chaplain. He served 10 years in the US Navy, and began his career in Cuba, and came home from Vietnam. He is currently serving as Chaplain for Vietnam Veterans of America, Chapter 317 in Kansas City, where he makes his home with his wife Susan. He also serves as Chaplain for One Community Hospice which honors Veterans and families who they serve. He has received Presidential Service Awards for more than 33,000 hours for Fire, Police and Military personnel.

Doc is president of Celebration of Life Counseling and Consulting and has spent decades helping couples achieve good spiritual and mental health in their marriages. He taught FOCIS (Focus on Children In Separation) classes for family court for couples going through divorce with custodial children so he's well equipped to help with issues involving child custody and co-parenting.

He has previously published "The Unhooked Celebration", a book for people recovering from nicotine addiction. In addition to owning several businesses in his time, he served as Clinical Director of Addiction Recovery and Homeless Services for a local mental health organization, has served as minister in three churches, and been a public speaker for 50 years. Doc is a psychologist specializing in addiction, marriage, career development and business building for many years.

The book contains many tools and much wisdom, none of which came from any school, but rather from his personal journey to recover Dignity, Identity and Purpose from the wreckage of a life no one would want to live. Following the guidance offered by this writing, you can turn a garbage can into a treasure chest.

He came home from Vietnam as a single parent, raising two small sons, and building businesses because after the war, no one wanted to hire Vietnam Veterans. Instead of folding up like a cheap card table, Doc started two businesses, and became very successful by knowing how to treat people. In the addition field, he created programs for recovering addicts to help them put their problem into remission and find a new and useful way to live. His career development program was given much credit for a lot of people learning how to re-enter society.